THE WORLD AT WAR
WORLD WAR II

Women at War

Heinemann Library
Chicago, Illinois

. . . . Brenda Williams

For more information address the publisher:
Heinemann Library, 100 N. LaSalle, Suite 1200,
Chicago, IL 60602

Editorial: Andrew Farrow and Dan Nunn
Design: Lucy Owen and Tokay Interactive Ltd
  (www.tokay.co.uk)
Picture Research: Hannah Taylor and Sally
  Claxton
Production: Duncan Gilbert

Originated by Repro Multi Warna
Printed and bound in China by
  WKT Company Limited

10 09 08 07 06
10 9 8 7 6 5 4 3 2 1

Library of Congress Cataloging-in-Publication Data

Williams, Brenda.
  Women at war / Brenda Williams.
    p. cm. -- (World at war-- World War II)
  Includes bibliographical references and index.
  ISBN 1-4034-6197-X (library binding-hardcover)
  1. World War, 1939-1945--Women.
  2. World War, 1939-1945--Participation, Female.
  3. World War, 1939-1945--War work.
  I. Title. II. Series.
  D810.6.W7W537 2005
  940.53'082--dc22
                          2005014759

Acknowledgments
The publishers would like to thank the following
for permission to reproduce photographs:

Australian War Memorial p. **22**; Corbis pp. **4**, **5**
(Hulton Deutsch Collection), **7 bottom** (Condé
Nast Archive), **16**, **18 bottom**, **19 top** (Hulton
Deutsch Collection), **25 top** (Hulton Deutsch
Collection), **28** (Hulton Deutsch Collection);
Getty Images pp. **9** (Hulton Archive), **10 top**
(Hulton Archive), **17** (Hulton Archive), **24**
(Hulton Archive), **27 top** (Hulton Archive);
Imperial War Museum pp. **10 bottom**, **11 top**,
21; Mary Evans Picture Library p. **13**; National
Army Museum p. **23 bottom**; Popperfoto pp. **6**,
12, **14**, **15 left**; Redferns Music Picture Library
p. **25 bottom**; Source unknown p. **15 right**;
The Art Archive pp. **19 bottom** (NARA), **27
bottom**; Topfoto.co.uk pp. **7 top** (Public Record
Office/HIP), **11 bottom** (Public Record
Office/HIP), **18 top** (Public Record Office/HIP),
26 (The Lord Price Collection); Topham
Picturepoint pp. **8**, **20**, **23 top**.

Cover photograph of Wrens fitting smoke floats
to a trainer aircraft at a Fleet Air Arm station,
1942, reproduced with permission of Popperfoto.

Every effort has been made to contact copyright
holders of any material reproduced in this book.
Any omissions will be rectified in subsequent
printings if notice is given to the publishers.

The paper used to print this book comes from
sustainable resources.

CONTENTS

Some words are shown in bold, **like this**. You can find out what they mean by looking in the glossary.

WAR BREAKS OUT

On September 1, 1939, German armies invaded Poland. World War II had begun. In this war women fought, worked, suffered, and died alongside men. Millions of women faced dangers and challenges with courage.

By 1940, German armies had conquered most of Europe, and in 1941 attacked the Soviet Union. In December 1941, Japan attacked the U.S. naval base at Pearl Harbor in Hawaii, and the United States joined the war. The global war made millions of women **refugees**. Many more faced hardship and danger in **occupied countries**.

Women go to war

The **Allies** summoned all of their people to fight in the war. Millions of men left home to join the army, navy, and air forces. Thousands of women also went into uniform. Millions of other women took over jobs that had usually been done by men—in **civil defense**, in factories and shipyards, in transportation, and on farms. Many young women left home for the first time in their lives.

▲ Bus and train stations were the scenes of many partings. The war meant years of separation. Many men were killed, and many wives became war **widows**.

Eyewitness

Most people heard the news of war in 1939 on the radio. A seventeen-year-old student-teacher in Essex, England, listened in the staff room at her school. News of the German bombing attacks on Poland reached the children. When she asked a class of thirteen- to fourteen-year-olds why they were not as well behaved as usual, one girl answered, "Well, miss, you see, we might not be here next week."

Adapted from a diary entry, September 1, 1939.

September 1, 1939
Germany invades Poland. Britain and France tell Germany to halt or face war. Germany does not reply.

September 3, 1939
Britain and France declare war on Germany. At 11:15 a.m. in Britain, many women are cooking Sunday lunch. Air raid **sirens** sound, but it is a false alarm.

September 3, 1939
Australia and New Zealand join the war on Britain's side. Canada joins on September 10.

Eyewitness

"I was standing on the carpet when the Pearl Harbor announcement was made ... I can remember looking at the carpet and thinking my life would never be the same again."

American teenager Nancy Potter

▲ As German armies swept through Europe, women and children became refugees. Thousands took to the roads in whatever vehicles they could find to seek safety from the fighting.

Waiting and wondering

Many married women were left to raise families while men were away in the armed forces. Wives and mothers dreaded the **telegram**, letter, or phone call with news that a husband or son serving in the armed forces was dead or missing. Many men did not return from the war.

Although only women in the Soviet Union actually fought in battles, many other women showed tremendous courage. In many countries, women worked, shopped, and cooked as usual. But at night bombs fell around their homes. World War II brought mass bombing from the air for the first time, and a bomb falling on a street killed women alongside men. Even when there were no bombs, women had to cope with shortages, **rationing**, learning new skills, and running a home alone. The "Home Front" was their battleground.

September 1939	April–June 1940	December 7, 1941
Thousands of British women and children are evacuated from cities to the countryside.	German armies overrun Norway, Denmark, the Netherlands, Belgium, and France. More than 300,000 Allied soldiers are rescued from Dunkirk in France.	The Japanese attack the U.S. Navy base at Pearl Harbor, Hawaii. The United States declares war the next day.

Making Do

In many countries, factories switched from peacetime production to making guns, planes, tanks, and uniforms. There was soon a shortage of many items, such as food, fuel, and clothes. Stores had much less to offer, and women managed with what they could buy, mend, or make themselves.

Rationing and recycling

Governments began to ration things. Rationing meant that families could only buy small amounts of certain goods. Stores would only sell rationed items if the shopper had a special coupon to buy that item. Some of the things rationed in the United States were food, gasoline, shoes, refrigerators, and tires. So people recycled lots of things. For example, governments gave women tips on how to use old clothes to make new clothes. Women knitted socks and scarves, patched old clothes, and mended worn sheets.

People also recycled rubber, newspapers, tin cans, and even old Civil War cannons!

▼ Hopeful shoppers gathered outside any store that had something to sell. Sometimes people complained, but most of them knew rationing was needed to help the war effort.

▶ This leaflet shows a wartime advertising slogan aimed at women, "Make-do and Mend." A character called "Mrs. Sew-and-Sew" showed British women "How to Patch Elbows and Trousers" or "How to Patch a Shirt." Shirts were easy to repair, said Mrs. Sew-and-Sew, because you could cut off a piece that didn't show to patch a hole.

MAKE-DO AND MEND

says Mrs. Sew-and-Sew

ISSUED BY THE BOARD OF TRADE

In the News

Advertising slogans aimed at women included:

- "Use it up, wear it out, make it do!"
- "Make do with less!"
- "Food is a weapon—don't waste it!"

◀ Schoolgirls and women in the United States and Canada knitted warm socks and scarves for servicemen. They also collected used clothes to send to people in **Allied** countries. There were fewer new clothes in stores because many factories had switched to making army uniforms, belts, boots, and other war materials.

DANGER FROM THE AIR

World War II was the first war in which mass air attacks were made on cities. In these attacks, women were on the front line.

Great Britain's Blitz

In Britain, the raids during the **Blitz** of 1940–1941 were a frightening time for millions of people. German bombers often attacked by night, when streets were darkened in the **blackout**. This meant that many families went without enough sleep. Women living through the noise and shock of an air raid tried to keep calm, to comfort frightened children, and to act normally. It was a great strain, and an experience few ever forgot.

Courage at Pearl Harbor

Though U.S. cities prepared for air raids, Japan and Germany had no bombers able to reach the United States. However, women at military bases in war zones were often in danger. For example, U.S. Army and Navy nurses were on duty when Japanese planes launched from aircraft carriers bombed Pearl Harbor in 1941. First Lieutenant Annie Fox, Chief Nurse at Hickam Field base, helped treat hundreds of injured men. For her "fine example of calmness, courage, and leadership" she was awarded the Purple Heart, a medal given only for outstanding behavior in wartime. She was the first of many U.S. Army nurses to be honored.

▲ This British couple's house was bombed in an air raid. Some "bombed-out" families went to live with relatives or neighbors. Others were given temporary shelter in rest centers and **billets**. Many soon moved back into fixed-up homes.

8

September 1940	November 1940–May 1941	December 1941
The Blitz on London begins. Many British women become air raid wardens.	The bombing of British cities is at its worst. Ports such as Liverpool and industrial centers such as Coventry are badly hit.	U.S. families begin hanging blackout curtains. These are so enemy bombers cannot see lighted buildings at night.

▲ In December 1941, U.S. women firefighters worked hard after Japan's air attack on Pearl Harbor, Hawaii. The naval base and surrounding airfields were left ablaze, with burning ships, wrecked planes, and more than 2,000 people killed.

Terrors of mass bombing

Women in Germany and Japan suffered greatly from 1942 until 1945 as Allied aircraft bombed German and Japanese cities. In mass raids on the German cities of Cologne, Hamburg, and Dresden, thousands of women were killed or injured, and many more were made homeless. In 1945 the Allies dropped the first atomic bombs, on the Japanese cities of Hiroshima and Nagasaki. Both cities were almost totally destroyed.

Eyewitness

Takeharu Terao was a student science-teacher assigned to war work in Hiroshima, Japan. Takeharu survived the atomic bomb attack on August 6, 1945.

"I witnessed a yellowish-scarlet plume rising like a candle high in the sky surrounded by pitch black swirling smoke. At the same moment ... houses lifted a little and then crashed down to the ground, like dominos. It was just like a white wave coming towards me while standing on the beach."

9

February 19, 1942

Japanese planes bomb Darwin, the first air raid on an Australian city. More than 240 are killed.

May 1942

Over 1,000 British bombers attack the German city of Cologne, which suffers more than 250 raids during the war.

February 1945

The German city of Dresden is devastated by a "fire-storm" started by Allied bombing. In March 1945, Tokyo in Japan suffers similar destruction.

Air Raids

Governments tried to be prepared for air attacks. This was called "civil defense." Families were taught how to use air raid shelters and gas masks (in case poison gas bombs were dropped). Women and men were trained to fight fires, rescue victims from bombed buildings, and give first aid to the injured. Air raid sirens would warn people of danger.

Air raid precautions

It was the job of air raid wardens to check each neighborhood to make sure no houses were showing lights in the blackout. There were no air raids in the United States, but at least everybody was prepared.

In Europe during air raids, people crowded into public shelters, big enough for hundreds of families. In cities such as Berlin in Germany and London in Britain, thousands of people spent nights in the underground subway stations. Many families had small air raid shelters in their gardens and backyards.

▲ Many U.S. cities also used underground subway stations as air raid shelters. These people are taking cover in a subway station in New York.

After a raid, wardens reported bomb damage and any unexploded bombs. Many women drove ambulances. And rest centers and portable kitchens were run by women volunteers, who served drinks, sandwiches, and soup to victims and rescuers.

▶ Women served in civil defense during the Blitz on Great Britain. They crewed **searchlight batteries**, flew **barrage balloons**, and directed **anti-aircraft guns** and fighter pilots to shoot down enemy bombers.

Eyewitness

Takeo Ikuma was a schoolboy in Kobe, Japan, in June 1945:

"The bombers came over in broad daylight, big silver aircraft floating through the sky. At first the smoke from the bombings hung in the air, rising slowly. But then the wind came up and the fires began to spread."

▲ Air raids meant nervous nights in shelters. Women made drinks and sandwiches, and tried to get children to sleep or read stories to calm them while bombs exploded above their heads.

In the News

"A few Eastern cities have recently heard the roar of a new siren whose wail is the loudest sustained sound ever produced by man. When the siren opens up, its cry is equal to the sound of 1,000 large symphony orchestras all playing at once."

This quotation comes from the Science News Letter of May 23, 1942. The siren was tested in New York city. It was designed to be heard above the noise of cities, so that people would be warned of air raids.

LOOKOUT IN THE BLACKOUT

UNTIL YOUR EYES GET USED TO THE DARKNESS **TAKE IT EASY**

▶ Governments published many posters about civil defense and air raids. This poster warned people to be careful until their eyes got used to the darkness of the blackout.

WAR WORK

Allied governments needed women to work alongside men making weapons. U.S. factories were soon employing thousands of women who had never worked before. And more women did the jobs that men used to do.

Joining the war effort

Between 1940 and 1944, the number of working women in the United States increased by over 50 percent. Typical was Almira Bondelid of San Diego, who left her retail job to work for a company that made aircraft, where she helped build B-24 Liberator bombers.

Marie Owens worked at the Huntsville Arsenal, in Alabama, making **munitions**. Her husband was in the U.S. Army. She told a reporter: "I am interested in carrying on here while the boys do the fighting over there ... The harder I work for them here, the sooner they will come home." This attitude was common among women in all countries at war.

Happy at work?

Movies, newspapers, and magazines showed women factory workers in pants and headscarves, smiling as they made tanks and planes. Workers were heard cheerfully singing along to radio programs.

▲ Factories hummed busily day and night to produce planes, guns, uniforms, and other war materials. Women learned new skills. Some worked alongside men, but others replaced men who had gone to join the armed forces.

1939

The German government awards "Mother's Cross" medals to women who have big families. Hitler thinks women should be mothers, not factory workers.

May 1940

The British government increases the working week in aircraft factories to 70 hours for each worker.

March 1941

More daycare centers are provided to help British working women with children.

Women at work

- Roughly 12 million American women were working in 1940 (in peacetime). By 1944, the number at work had risen to over 18 million.

- By 1943, 90 percent of single women and 80 percent of married women in Britain were doing war work or were in the armed services.

- **Nazi** Germany did not call up women for factory work until 1943. Hitler thought that German women should raise children at home, not do "men's work."

- However, the Nazis did force women captives from occupied countries to work in their factories.

▲ In many countries, women firefighters like these risked being killed or wounded by buildings falling on them, or unexploded bombs blowing up without any warning.

In real life, women found factory life exhausting. Many worked ten-hour **shifts** for five or six days a week. After work, they had children to care for, and a home to keep going. Young women who had never been away from home before went to work, often to a city they did not know.

Different pay

Almost all women workers grumbled that they were paid less than men doing the same job. On average, women workers made as little as one-third of what male workers did. This was very unfair, because the government paid companies more money for employing women!

13

December 1941	1942	February 1943
In Britain, women ages 20–30 have to register for war work. By 1942, 8.5 million women ages 19–46 have been registered.	The head of the U.S. War Manpower Commission states that "no women responsible for the care of young children" should be made to work.	Germany calls up all men and women aged 16–65 for war work. By 1944, women make up one-third of Britain's engineering workforce.

Women Build Aircraft

Aircraft were a vital part of the war effort. Women helped to build them. In 1942, U.S. President Franklin D. Roosevelt called on U.S. factories to build 60,000 aircraft per year. Few people believed it was possible. But in 1943, U.S. factories built almost 86,000 planes. The next year they built more than 96,000.

Many factories had stopped making peacetime goods. Instead, workers previously trained in making things like furniture or vacuum cleaners now had to assemble everything from radars to airplanes. Workers quickly learned new skills. And work went on in spite of air raids.

▲ Women handled heavy machinery and assembled small parts for precision equipment. This woman is working on a cylinder block, part of an engine for a propeller-driven fighter or bomber plane. Posters in factories urged workers to do their job faster and build more planes.

In the News

Newspapers and magazines persuaded women to work in factories. Newspapers carried ads for jobs in other states. Women's magazines said that making a bomb was like following a cooking recipe. They said that cutting parts for airplanes was like cutting cloth to make a dress. African Americans and other minorities found it easier to get jobs, too. Many people moved to cities like Detroit, Michigan, and Long Beach, California.

Eyewitness

Muriel Simkin worked in a munitions (weapons) factory in England. She remembered air raids.

"On one occasion a bomb hit the factory before we were given permission to go to the shelter. The paint department went up. I saw several people flying through the air and I just ran home ... It was a terrible job but we had no option ... We were risking our lives in the same way as the soldiers were."
Interviewed in *Voices from the Past: The Blitz* (1987)

We Can Do It!

WAR PRODUCTION CO-ORDINATING COMMITTEE

▲ Millions of American women worked in airplane factories. They earned the nickname "Rosie the Riveter." Rosie was a character in a government advertising campaign.

▲ Sewing silk for parachutes. Any mistake in packing a parachute and its long cords could cost the life of an airman leaping from a burning plane.

▼ This graph shows how the United States increased its aircraft production after it entered the war in 1941. It was soon building more planes than any other country.

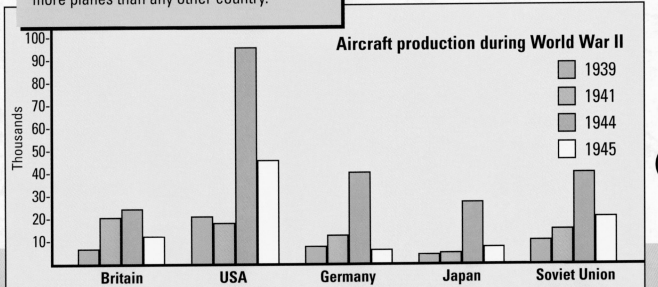

Aircraft production during World War II

Thousands

- 1939
- 1941
- 1944
- 1945

Britain   USA   Germany   Japan   Soviet Union

FEEDING THE FAMILY

Food was as important to the war effort as guns and planes. Farmers were urged to grow more food. In many countries women took over farming jobs that had been done by men.

Submarines and airplanes on both sides sank hundreds of enemy ships carrying food. The war destroyed fields and crops, and many people starved. Hunger was worst in China and in the Soviet Union, where many farmers were driven from the land by the Japanese and German invasions. In occupied countries, the Nazis kept the best food for themselves. By 1945, many Japanese were surviving on one meal a day of rice mixed with soy beans, or dumplings made from ground wheat and grass.

Rationing for all

Women had to cook and eat whatever food they could find. In some countries there was food rationing. Everyone was issued a ration book. Stores could only sell rationed foods to people who had coupons from the book. The United States government brought in some rationing in 1942. It controlled the sale of meat, eggs, sugar, coffee, and other foods. There was also a shortage of cooking oil. Anybody who broke the rationing rules was punished.

▶ Shoppers in the United States wait in a line to buy rations of sugar. People were not used to waiting to buy food.

September 1939	**January 1942**	**1942**
German submarines, called U-boats, begin sinking ships carrying food and other goods to Germany's enemies.	U-boats begin sinking hundreds of American ships before the U.S. Navy can protect them properly.	The Office of Price Administration sets up a rationing scheme. Coffee is one of the items rationed.

> ▶ The United States shipped tons of food to its Allies, like the Soviet Union and Great Britain. Shipments of square-sided cans of Spam, canned meat first sold in the United States in 1937, arrived along with powdered eggs, Hershey chocolate bars, chewing gum, and many other foods.

Staying healthy

In spite of shortages, most people kept healthy, and some people became overweight. Rationing did mean that everyone got a fair share of basic foods. Cooks were urged to try familiar foods in unfamiliar ways, such as making pot pies without meat, for example! Sugar was rationed, and jam and chocolate were treats.

In Germany, women made coffee from ground acorns, after supplies of imported coffee beans were stopped by the war.

Eyewitness

In the United States, Mary Gardner of Rhode Island (whose father fished for food) remembered her wartime diet, "we ate a lot of fish because meat was rationed ... you had to buy things that were going to stretch [make a lot of meals], maybe spaghetti, macaroni ... and mix it up with something else."

Quoted in *An Oral History of Rhode Island Women, South Kingstown High School*

February 1943	April 1943	1944-1945
U.S. shoppers are rationed to three pairs of new shoes a year. In Britain, the ration is one pair.	Meat, canned foods, and cheese are rationed in the United States.	"Victory gardens" at people's homes produce 40 percent of vegetables eaten in the United States.

Vegetables for Victory

Women were urged to "dig for victory." This meant growing vegetables in gardens, backyards, public parks—anywhere there was a patch of soil. Schools joined in, with children and teachers planting beans, tomatoes, potatoes, cabbages, and peas in what were called victory gardens. By 1945, victory gardens produced nearly half of the vegetables eaten in the United States.

Working on the land

To replace male farmworkers and make sure the harvest was collected, the government set up the U.S. Crop Corps. More than one million women joined a branch of the Crop Corps called the Women's Land Army (WLA). They were expected to be healthy and good at working with their hands. The WLA had its own uniform, though most women did not wear it. There were Land Armies in Australia and Britain also.

For a healthy, happy job

Join the
WOMEN'S LAND ARMY

For details:
APPLY TO NEAREST W.L.A. COUNTY OFFICE OR TO W.L.A. HEADQUARTERS 6 CHESHAM PLACE LONDON S.W.1

Issued by the Ministry of Agriculture and the Ministry of Labour and National Service

▼ This young boy is being handed his first ration book. To make up for the shortage of protein foods, such as meat, fish, and eggs (all rationed), mothers were encouraged to serve more vegetables.

▲ Posters like this showed happy workers enjoying harvest-time. Most young women, often from big cities, found farm work cold and wet, bruising, and back-aching. But they stuck with it. Many traveled from their homes each day, and returned at night. A few lived on the farms year round.

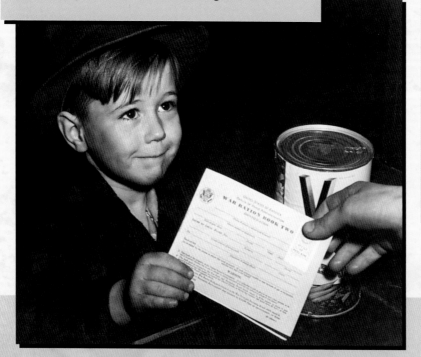

FEEDING THE FAMILY

◀ Women's Land Army members learned new skills, such as driving tractors. In the 1940s, many farmers still used horses, not tractors, and even machine-threshing (separating wheat grain from the stalks) needed up to twelve workers. Women had to do many different difficult and dirty jobs.

Posters

Posters and brochures urged women to grow food and use it carefully. They had slogans like:

- "Food is a Weapon: Don't Waste It"

- "Help Harvest War Crops: Join the U.S. Crop Corps"

- "Make Food Fight for Freedom by Eating Wisely"

- "Fish is a Fighting Food: We Need More"

GROW YOUR OWN *Be sure!*

GARDEN IN 1945 FOR VICTORY

▶ Americans needed to grow and preserve fruits and vegetables. A wartime slogan in the United States was "Grow your own. Be sure!" The message behind this was that home-grown vegetables were healthy and also helped the war effort. "Growing your own" was good for everyone.

WOMEN UNDER FIRE

Women served in armies, navies, and air forces, though few fought in combat. Some flew fighter and bomber planes. Others carried out dangerous missions behind enemy lines.

Women did many jobs in the forces. They were cooks, clerks, drivers, electricians, code experts, radio operators, pilots, parachute packers, and meteorologists (weather experts). A few became secret agents in occupied countries helping the **Resistance**. Only in the Soviet Union did women fight alongside, and against, men. More than half the 800,000 women in the Soviet Army served as machine-gunners, tank drivers, **snipers**, combat pilots, and medics. In World War II, roughly 400,000 women served in the U.S. armed forces.

Women pilots

American and most Allied women were not allowed to fly in combat, but they did pilot new aircraft from factories to air force bases. Two famous wartime pilots were 1930s air racer Jacqueline Cochran, who led the U.S. Women's Flying Training Detachment (WFTD), and Britain's Amy Johnson. In 1930 Johnson had flown solo from Britain to Australia. During the war she was killed while ferrying warplanes for Britain's Air Transport Auxiliary.

▶ Jacqueline Cochran (shown here after the war) won fame in the 1930s as a pilot in air races. During World War II she led the U.S. women pilots, or WASPs. After the war, she flew jets and became the fastest woman pilot in the world.

20

March 1941	April 1941	May 1942
Women join the new Women's Auxiliary Australian Air Force. About 27,000 have enlisted by 1945.	British women's services officially become part of the armed services, under the same military rules as men.	The Women's Army Auxiliary Corps (WAAC) is formed in the United States.

▶ A woman pilot with a British Royal Air Force plane. Women flew new planes from factories to air bases. They also helped flight-test equipment such as radios.

Women in Germany

The Nazis thought women should stay at home as mothers and homemakers and not wear the army uniform. Some Nazis even disapproved of women wearing pants! But this did not stop German women from doing war work as civilians. For example, pilot Hanna Reisch tested new, experimental warplanes. And she bravely flew messages in and out of Berlin during the battles in that city before Adolf Hitler's death in 1945.

In the News

In 1942, a War Department booklet told U.S. soldiers going to Britain, "British women have proved themselves in this war ... When you see a girl in uniform with a bit of ribbon [an award for good service] on her tunic, remember she didn't get it for knitting more socks than anyone else..."

Women in the armed forces

- U.S. Women's Army Corps (WAC). By 1944, there were roughly 100,000 WACs, over 15,000 serving overseas.

- U.S. Army and Navy nurses. In 1945 there were nearly 70,000 nurses in the armed forces.

- U.S. Marines. More than 20,000 women served with the U.S. Marine Corps.

- U.S. Women Accepted for Volunteer Emergency Service (WAVES). Over 100,00 women served in the U.S. Navy.

21

November 1942	1943	June 1944
SPARS, the Women's Reserve of the U.S. Coast Guard, is formed in the United States.	The U.S. Women's Flying Training Detachment (WFTD) merges with the Women's Auxiliary Ferrying Squadron to form the WASPs (Women Airforce Service Pilots).	Army nurses are among the first women in uniform to serve in Normandy, France, soon after the D-Day landings.

Captured by the Enemy

Working as a secret agent was one of the most dangerous jobs in wartime. There were no rules. A soldier in uniform, if captured, must be treated properly as a prisoner of war. A captured agent, with no uniform, could be shot as a spy. Defying the risks, brave women volunteered to parachute into occupied countries to help the resistance to the Nazis.

Women captives

Many other women, including civilians and nurses captured in New Guinea, Malaya, and the Philippines, were imprisoned or forced to work in labor camps by the Nazis and Japanese. In Europe, millions of Jewish children and women were put to death in **concentration camps** during the Holocaust.

In the News

"Few if any women have been decorated so highly for their exploits during the Second World War." The media praised Nancy Wake (then aged 91), who in 2004 was made a Companion of the Order of Australia. Honored for her wartime courage, she said modestly, "I hope I am worth it."

▲ Nancy Wake was born in New Zealand and raised in Australia. In 1939, she was living in France. She escaped to Great Britain, but parachuted back into occupied France as a secret agent. In France, she carried messages by bicycle and also **sabotaged** factories. The Germans nicknamed her the "White Mouse," because she was so hard to catch.

WOMEN UNDER FIRE

◀ Agent Odette Sansom (a French woman married to an Englishman) had the code name "Lise." In 1943 she was captured by the Germans, but this is what she thought of her captors: "They will kill me physically, but that's all. They won't win anything." She survived almost two years in a concentration camp, was honored after the war for her bravery, and died in 1995.

Profile of a secret agent

- Noor-un-Nisa Inayat Khan had American and Indian parents. Raised in France, she knew the language and the people.

- Trained as an agent in England, she was given the code name "Madeleine." She traveled with a radio hidden in a suitcase. Her job was to pass messages between England and the French Resistance.

- She was captured in 1943 by the **Gestapo**, tortured, and shot.

◀ Some women agents carried a small radio like this one, which could be hidden in a suitcase. Radio operators moved frequently, from house to house, because the Gestapo could trace messages sent from the same place night after night.

23

KEEP SMILING

Even in war, women still had some leisure time. News and entertainment came from radio, movies, newspapers, and magazines. Women did their best to keep spirits up, as entertainers and as family members.

Radio times

Not many people owned televisions, so most listened to the radio. People heard news reports and broadcasts by war leaders. President Franklin D. Roosevelt gave "Fireside Chats" to the American people. British Prime Minister Winston Churchill, whose mother was American, made many stirring speeches.

Both sides used **propaganda**. Radio broadcasts by "Lord Haw Haw" (speaking from Germany) and "Tokyo Rose" (from Japan) were full of boasts and threats. They caused more amusement than alarm. Many women listened to programs about current events and what might happen after the war.

Popular music and film

- Many women were fans of male "crooners" [singers] such as Bing Crosby and Frank Sinatra.

- There were many women stars too, such as Adelaide Hall, Judy Garland, Betty Grable, and Marlene Dietrich.

- Gracie Allen was a famous comedienne.

- Popular wartime films included *Gone With the Wind*, *The Wizard of Oz*, *Mrs. Miniver* (an American view of a British family at war), and Shakespeare's *Henry V*.

▲ People enjoyed dancing on weekends. Dance halls were always full, and dance bands were very popular. The Glenn Miller Army Air Force Band was the most famous band. It performed hundreds of concerts in Europe, many of them broadcast to millions of people on the radio.

July 1941
The "V for Victory" signal, "da-da-da-dah" (from Beethoven's 5th Symphony), is first used to introduce British news bulletins to occupied Europe.

February 1941
The United Service Organizations (USO) is formed. It sets up clubs where servicemen and women can dance, listen to music, read, and relax.

October 1942
British stores start selling cardboard wedding cakes after the government bans cake frosting.

◄ On holidays people remembered loved ones far away, and hoped that next year the war would be over. Some spent Christmas in air raid shelters.

▼ Adelaide Hall was a popular wartime singer.

Entertainment for all

Music and laughter helped to keep people happy. People hummed the latest hit tunes while they worked, and went to the movies to forget the war for a couple of hours.

Entertainers such as film star Betty Hutton and British singer Vera Lynn toured the war zones. And in battle zones around the world, women singers, dancers, and actresses performed to troops near the front line, even when bombs or shells started to fall nearby.

Letters and parties

Women also worked hard to keep up family **morale**. They wrote letters to husbands, sons, or brothers who were working or serving far from home. They organized birthday, holiday, and homecoming parties. The best parties broke out in streets and homes in 1945. On VE Day (May 8) and VJ Day (August 14), people celebrated the end of the war, first in Europe and then in the Pacific.

Eyewitness

Jean Pountney went into the town of Melton Mowbray, in England, for dances on Wednesday nights and met American soldiers, called **GIs**.

"The Americans had all the latest records. I'd seen jiving [a dance] before, but not the way they did it. I was dancing with one chap and suddenly he swept me off my feet!"

25

1942	1943	December 1944
To help U.S. troops arriving in Britain feel at home, American Red Cross women serve coffee and doughnuts from trucks.	U.S. First Lady Eleanor Roosevelt tours Australia and the South Pacific to support U.S. soldiers.	American bandleader Glenn Miller is presumed killed when his plane disappears on a flight from England to France.

Love and Marriage

Many women made lasting friendships and found lifelong partners during the war. Men and women often met and found love by chance—working together, waiting for a bus or train, or getting lost in the blackout. And many married couples were separated during the war, so lots of children grew up without fathers around. The war put a lot of pressure on family life and caused thousands of marriages to break up.

KEEP SMILING

▶ A homecoming in Britain in 1945. Some separated couples managed to meet on occasional weekends, but for others, years passed before they were reunited. Letters were the only way to keep in touch.

GI brides

From 1942, thousands of American troops, nicknamed "GIs," served in North Africa, Britain, Europe, Australia, and the Pacific Ocean. Many foreign women married American servicemen. Most then went to live in the United States. Newspapers called them "GI brides."

▶ Couples who married during the war often had to arrange a quick and simple wedding. Then the bride or groom would have to go back to the military or war work, and they might not see each other for many months. Some wartime marriages did not last very long.

A threat to family life?

Many women ran a home and worked long hours in factories. They also did volunteer activities, such as selling war bonds (to raise money for the war), collecting unwanted clothing, and tending vegetable gardens. Not everyone thought this was a good thing.

Critics claimed that women at work let their children run wild. And many said they disapproved of the "new habit" of women going dancing and to bars on their own.

▶ Couples separated by the war often shared favorite songs. Hit tunes were sold on records and in songbooks, like these.

THE IMPACT OF WAR

World War II had an enormous impact on society. For women who lost family and friends, life would never be the same. They were left with sad memories. But not all memories were painful. Many women had fun, made new friends, travelled the world, and learned new skills.

Many men who worked alongside women appreciated their abilities and courage. Even so, when peace came in 1945, women still faced an uphill struggle for equal pay and fair treatment at work.

The war's legacy

Today, women fly fighter planes and command warships. Women hold top jobs in government and industry. World War II helped bring about the "women's rights" movement because millions of women at war had gained confidence and ambition. In 1940 the editor of an aircraft magazine had written: "... there are millions of women who could do useful jobs in war. But the trouble is ... so many insist on wanting to do jobs which they are quite incapable of doing."

By 1945, most people knew that women were capable of doing almost anything.

Eyewitnesses

"The girls lived like men, fought like men and, alas, some of them died like men. Unarmed, they showed great courage."

Lt. General Sir Frederick Pile, commander of British anti-aircraft defenses.

"This war more than any other war in history is a woman's war."

John G. Winant, U.S. ambassador to Britain during the war.

▲ VE Day, Tuesday May 8, 1945, marked the end of the war in Europe. By August, with the defeat of Japan, the war was finally over. Nancy Harjan was seventeen years old. "I was totally blown away by how quickly our former enemies became our friends. I couldn't understand that. I began to ask, what was it all about?"

TIMELINE

1939

September 1 Germany invades Poland.

September 3 Great Britain and France declare war on Germany. Thousands of troops leave home to join the armed forces. In Britain, many mothers have already parted with children who have been evacuated to the countryside.

1940

January Butter, bacon, and eggs are rationed in Britain.

April Germany invades Denmark and Norway.

May Germany invades Belgium, the Netherlands, and France. Many women become refugees. Women join the Resistance.

June Italy joins Germany in the Axis alliance. France surrenders.

July The German air force begins attacks on Britain. Women help in the defense.

September The Blitz on Britain begins. Women serve as air raid wardens.

1941

March Australia recruits more women to its armed forces.

April Germany invades Greece and Yugoslavia.

May The United States begins shipping food rations to Britain.

June Germany invades the Soviet Union. Soviet women fight alongside men in the army.

December 7 The Japanese attack on Pearl Harbor brings the United States into the war. In December, Japan also invades Malaya, the Philippines and other islands in the Pacific. Women there suffer badly.

1942

January–February Singapore and the Philippines fall to the Japanese, who threaten Australia.

May The U.S. Army women's branch, the WAAC, is set up.

June 8 Two Japanese submarines shell the Australian cities of Sydney and Newcastle.

August U.S. troops land in the Solomon Islands, at Guadalcanal.

September The Germans and Russians fight for Stalingrad, in the Soviet Union.

October–November The Allies win the Battle of El Alamein in North Africa.

November Coffee is rationed in the United States. The U.S. government calls for more women to join the armed forces.

December Thousands of U.S. troops are away from home for the first time at Christmas.

1943

February The Allied bombing of Germany increases. German women are called up for war work.

February A German army surrenders at Stalingrad.

May The Allies drive the Axis forces out of North Africa.

July The Allies land in Sicily, Italy. The Allies also begin the recapture of islands from the Japanese in the Pacific.

September U.S. First Lady Eleanor Roosevelt visits Pearl Harbor, Hawaii.

1944

June Women in Britain experience frightening new air attacks by V-1 flying bombs.

June 6 D-Day; Allied armies land in France to begin the liberation of Western Europe. Women nurses follow the invasion troops.

August 25 France's capital city, Paris, is liberated.

October The Allies begin the recapture of the Philippines.

December German armies attack U.S. forces in the Ardennes. The huge battle lasts for two months. More American soldiers are killed than in any other battle of World War II.

1945

January Many German families are near starvation.

February Fierce fighting after U.S. forces land on Iwo Jima, close to Japan's main islands. Many Japanese kill themselves rather than surrender.

February 14 The German city of Dresden is destroyed by bombing raids.

April Survivors are rescued from Nazi concentration camps, where millions of people have been put to death.

April 30 Hitler kills himself in Berlin as Soviet armies capture the German capital city.

May 7 Germany surrenders. Millions of women are among the refugees.

August 6 Allies drop an atomic bomb on the Japanese city of Hiroshima, and another on Nagasaki three days later. Japan stops fighting.

August 14 Crowds celebrate V-J (Victory over Japan) Day. The war is over. Families are reunited and people begin rebuilding their lives.

GLOSSARY

Allies Britain, France, Canada, Australia, the Soviet Union, the United States, and other countries that fought together against Germany, Italy, and Japan

anti-aircraft gun big gun that fires shells thousands of yards into the air to hit or scare off enemy planes

barrage balloons large balloons on wire cables, used as a defense against low-flying aircraft

battery group of guns or searchlights

billet temporary home, usually where people share another family's house

blackout measures to reduce all lights at night in order to hide possible targets from enemy bombers

Blitz the German bombing attack on London and other British cities

civil defense arrangements to protect towns and cities from enemy attack, especially from the air

concentration camp prison camp in which captives are kept without proper housing, food, or medical treatment

Gestapo German secret police who hunted Allied agents and Resistance fighters

GI nickname for U.S. soldiers; short for General Issue (referring to standard clothes given to all soldiers)

morale spirit of the people in a country at war

munitions ammunition, explosives, guns, and other combat material

Nazi member of the National Socialist German Workers' Party, led by Adolf Hitler

occupied country a country that is conquered and then ruled by an invader

propaganda control of information in the media designed to show your side in a good light and the enemy in a bad way

rationing government control of the sale of food, fuel, clothes, and other goods

refugee homeless person fleeing in search of safety during wartime

Resistance members of an organization fighting enemy forces that have occupied their country

sabotage to break equipment, slow down work in a factory, or in other ways harm an enemy's war effort

searchlight large electric light used to find enemy planes in the night sky, so they can be shot down

shift period of work in a factory, usually about eight hours but often longer in wartime

siren device that makes a loud wailing noise as a warning

sniper sharpshooter trained to shoot at enemy soldiers, usually from a concealed position

telegram urgent communication sent by phone line, but delivered to an address as a short printed message

widow a woman whose husband has died

FINDING OUT MORE

If you are interested in finding out more about World War II, here are some more books you might find useful.

Further reading

Your local public library's adult section should have plenty of war books, including books about what it was like to be a woman during World War II. Written by people who were actually there, such books will give you an idea of what ordinary people thought about the war and their part in it.

Books for younger readers

Adams, Simon. *World War II.* New York: DK Children, 2004.

Ambrose, Stephen E. *The Good Fight.* New York: Simon & Schuster, 2001.

Colman, Penny. *Rosie the Riveter: Women Working on the Homefront in World War II.* New York: Knopf, 1995.

Dolan, Edward F. *America in WWII – 1943.* Brookfield: Millbrook, 1992.

Josephson, Judith Pinkerton. *Growing Up in World War II: 1941–1945.* Minneapolis: Lerner, 2002.

King, David C. *World War II Days.* New York: Wiley, 2000.

Kuhn, Betsy. *Angels of Mercy: The Army Nurses of World War II.* Illinois: Atheneum, 1999.

Panchyk, Richard. *WWII for Kids.* Chicago: Chicago Review Press, 2002.

Tanaka, Shelley. *Attack on Pearl Harbor.* New York: Hyperion, 2001.

Also the Heinemann Library *Holocaust* and *Witness to History* series (several titles).

INDEX